Year-Round
Entertaining

Easy and Creative Solutions

Mary Forsell

Photography by Luciana Pampalone

Styling by Susan George

p

This is a Parragon Publishing Book
Conceived and produced by Glitterati Incorporated/www.GlitteratiIncorporated.com

First published in 2006 by
Parragon Publishing
Queen Street House
4 Queen Street
Bath BA1 1HE, UK

Copyright © 2006 by Glitterati Incorporated
Text by Mary Forsell
Photographs by Luciana Pampalone
Styling by Susan George

Design by Anthia Papadopoulos

ISBN: 978-1-4054-7769-7

Dedication…
For Elizabeth Forsell, who is always entertaining.

Acknowledgments
Tony Cenicola, for putting up with "the box of reference materials."
Marta Hallett, for conceiving the idea and making it all happen.

Year-Round
Entertaining

Easy and Creative Solutions

Mary Forsell

Photography by Luciana Pampalone

Styling by Susan George

Contents

Chapter 1: Basics

For some of us, entertaining comes naturally. People can drop in and we'll always have something on hand. The secret to being a good host isn't charm, it's planning ahead.

There are two basic scenarios to entertaining: The first is that unexpected guests drop by and you have to pull together an informal gathering on the spot. The other scenario is the invitation, which enables you to plan ahead, including making a shopping list, placing food orders, reserving rental equipment, and planning the décor—including making sure you have enough seating.

Begin planning in advance. About a week in advance, shop for party items, frozen food, canned goods, and ingredients to make dishes. Prepare whatever dishes possible in advance. Check liquor supply and frequently used items and add whatever is necessary to the shopping list. This is also the time to buy candles and other décor and make sure table linens are cleaned and pressed. About three to four days in advance, you can move on to polishing silver (if it's a fancy party), cleaning seldom used dishes, making sure glassware is clean, and making food that can be frozen or will keep to the day of the party.

Two days before, clean the house, buy ice, do that last-minute ingredient check. On the day before the party, finish as much of the cooking as possible, rearrange furniture as needed, clear room for guests' coats, set up the bar, and have your coffee and tea service ready to roll. That means on the day of the party, you'll be ready to cook, put that white wine on ice and arrange your flowers. Just before the party, set out cheese or other nonperishable snacks, open red wine and mix first batch of cocktails or juices. Now relax and enjoy yourself (really)!

Informal vs. Formal Entertaining

Whether your guests are wearing tuxedos or jeans, there are certain "rules" that should be observed. First, be sure they're mixed and matched well. Try to establish what your guests have in common when you make your introductions. Just a tidbit of information can become a lively discussion after you've excused yourself. If someone seems left adrift, engage him in conversation and gently lead him to another guest with whom you think he shares an interest.

Periodically ask your guests if they need another drink or a glass of something else. Always provide nonalcoholic drinks such as seltzer, soda, juice, or sparking cider. And if it's a sitdown affair, once everyone is happily seated, don't delay picking up your fork and asking your guests to begin.

A Cook's Tools

If you're entertaining only small groups—for instance, six or eight guests—your family-sized utensils will serve their purpose. But if you're going for larger gatherings, say twelve or more, then you're going to need bigger supplies: party-sized casserole dishes, covered roasting pan, oversize soup tureens, holiday turkey platters.

Note that, except for cast-iron skillets, it is important that saucepans and pots are nonreactive stainless steel or ceramic to prevent chemical changes that occur when you're cooking with acidic ingredients like citrus juice, wine, vinegar, and tomatoes. Cooking with aluminum can alter flavors.

Everyone has a different cooking style, but it's undeniable that certain pieces of equipment make food preparation both faster and simpler. Why do things the old-fashioned way when there are short cuts. Among the equipment and handy gadgets that cooks swear by:

*Grater/Zestier
Go with the microplane rather than the boxy kind because it has many smaller holes. Truly, it's the only way to get delicate gratings from citrus and parmigiana cheese

*Knives
Invest in a few high quality steel knives and have a steel or stone sharpener. Knives that one must have are a chef's knife, utility knife, paring knife, and bread knife

*Euro Peeler
Much better than a traditional vegetable peeler, it lets you go more quickly and doesn't get clogged

*Immersion Blender
A long wand with a blade, this portable blender can be inserted right into a pot to puree and makes cleanup MUCH easier

*Spice Grinder
Buy an inexpensive coffee grinder and use it just for this purpose

A Cook's Ingredients

Keep these pantry and fridge staples on hand, and you'll always be able to whip up something special.

*Salt-cured Anchovies
These can be used to flavor salad dressings (such as Caesar), in sauces as a secret ingredient that enhances other flavors

*Vinegars
Balsamic (the best have the designation "aceto balsamico tradizionale di Modena" on the label), sherry, and tarragon

*Canned Tomatoes
Those that come from San Marzano, Italy are best. They're plum tomatoes available whole or crushed.

*Capers
Small addition that goes a long way

*Chipotle Peppers
Smoked jalapeno peppers come canned in a spicy sauce

*Eggs

*Extra Virgin Olive Oil

The best come form Italy, Spain, Greece, and France. Use it to finish dishes rather than as a cooking medium

*Five-Spice Powder
Chinese blend of cinnamon, cloves, fennel seed, star anise, and Szechuan peppercorns adds a lively spice

*Fresh Ginger

*Grapeseed Oil
A fabulous choice for sauteing because of its near invisible taste

*Israeli Couscous
It's actually a semolina paste that you can use in salads or add to soups

*Lemon Olive Oil
It's great to drizzle over seafood

*Olives
Whether you use them as an hors d'oeuvres or ingredients, they're indispensable. Green olives are harvested when grown but not ripe; black olives are ripened. Gaeta, Nicoise, Picholine, Moroccan, and Sicilian

*Pancetta
An Italian bacon, it's not smoked but cured in a combination of spices. You can use it in place of butter or oil and it freezes well

*Pasta
Imported dried Italian pastas are great in a pinch

*Pizza Dough

*Puff Pastry

*Rice
Especially arborio for creamy risotto

*Saffron
What would Spanish paella or French bouillabaisse be without it? Purchase threads rather than powdered

*Prepared Pasta Sauces

*Sea Salt

*Sesame Oil:
Essential to Asian dishes

*Soy Sauce
Also an Asian staple

*Onions and Garlic

*Stocks
Stocks can be time consuming to make, so buy unsalted chicken and vegetable stocks from the store and enrich it with aromatic vegetables

*Truffle oil
This can made by infusing olive oil with truffle and should be used sparingly

*Tuna packed in olive oil (good in a pinch)

*Variety of good quality cheeses such as Parmigiana Reggiano, and feta

*Walnut Oil
Adds a lively kick to soup

*Wine
For cooking and drinking

In a Pinch: Tips and Shortcuts

FOOD

Even busy people can cook from scratch by planning their kitchen time wisely and relying on today's convenience products.

Here are some of our favorite ways to make home cooking and entertaining quicker and easier than ever.

*Before starting any meal preparation, read all recipes thoroughly. You'll also save time by assembling ingredients and utensils before you begin.

*Rely on boneless, thin cuts of meat and poultry that cook quickly—usually in less than twenty minutes

*Convenience products give you a jump on cooking by doing some of the work for you. Items such as shredded cheese, minced fresh garlic, frozen chopped onions, precut vegetables, refrigerated doughs, and cubed meat for stir fries or stews often cost more, but the time saved may be worth the extra cost to you.

*Add favorite ingredients to quick-fix products. For instance, spread purchased cheesecake with seedless raspberry preserves and decorate with fresh fruit. Or make a simple main dish by stir-frying stirps of pork or beef, then adding a package of frozen Oriental vegetables and serving over rice.

*Make a mix unique with a few tasty additions. Top brownie mix batter with almond brickle pieces and chocolate pieces before baking. Ad orange or lemon peel or nuts to sweet muffins. Add chili peppers and shredded cheese to corn muffins.

*Go with flavor-building ingredients like infused oils and compound butters. For instance drizzling orange oil into a carrot-saffron soup. To be good, a dish doesn't have to have a ton of ingredients. Instead, simplicity can enhance the taste of food.

DECORATIONS

Equally important as the food you create for dining is the mood you set. Just a few minutes spent lighting candles or putting a favorite memento at the center of your dining table will make guests feel more than welcome and enhance the experience.

Here are a few staples to pull out in a second to create an inviting environment:

*Candles by the dozen

 Votives, tapers, pillars; dripless kinds for sconces and chandeliers

*Mirrors

 They create dramatic centerpieces with objects placed on top

*Throws, camp blankets

 To dress up the living room or set a picnic mood outdoors

*Mosquito netting for quick canopies

*Extra sets of inexpensive flatware, plates, and wineglasses

*Wooden, wicker, and silver trays for serving cocktails and hors d'oeuvres

*Cachepots, urns, and vases for instant floral displays—scour secondhand stores

*Paper lanterns from the Oriental supply store

 They're inexpensive but dramatic for creating a mood

*Strings of white lights

 Weave them through your potted plants, decorate the deck

Chapter 2. Come for

One of the simplest ways to entertain is the cocktail party. With a well-stocked bar and some cleverly devised hors d'oeuvres, you can pull off a party to remember without the need for a full sit-down meal or hosting an all-day event.

It could be as casual as, "Come for drinks and nibbles after work," or as formal as waiters passing hors d'oeuvres from trays. Somewhere in between is the spontaneous party. If that's your style, you'll want to have on hand a number of staples like hard salami and blue cheese, bread sticks, olives, sour cream for mixing with fresh herbs, and traditional cafe aperitifs that live permanently on a rolling cart.

Cocktails

Appetizer Wisdom

You want your guests to be wowed and delighted by the food. But, at the same time, you don't have an unlimited budget. There are some sneaky tricks of the trade you can employ to give your party panache without the price tag. Let's say you want to serve shrimp—an expensive food. Instead of placing out a heaping mound on a "help yourself" buffet, divvy them up on individual bamboo skewers. Add sophistication with exotic eats like egg-plant "caviar" and Vietnamese summer rolls wrapped in rice paper—inexpensive yet impressive.

Streamline your presentation. By only offering finger foods like parmesan chips, Jamaican jerk chicken on skewers, or baby beef burgers and tiny sandwiches on interesting breads, you will cut down on plates and flatware. Guests will feel more relaxed and free to mingle since they won't have to deal with utensils.

If you are planning on having waitstaff, save yourself a bundle by using a rolling cart. It requires just one person to push it, yet holds dozens of small plates that would take an army to pass out.

Cheese If You Please

A cheese tray is perhaps the easiest way to please a crowd. But it has to look as luscious as it tastes. Select cheeses with different flavors, shapes, textures, and colors. For instance, a rich Camembert and creamy Mascarpone would contrast with wedges of tangy gorgonzola.

Specialty cheeses, like peppered brie and muenster-cheddar, are another option. When pairing cheese with wine, remember, the more robust the cheese, the heartier the wine. For instance, sauvignon blanc or champagne with a young goat cheese or aged cheddar with cabernet.

Olives Anyone?

Olives are standard cocktail party fare. In Spain, they're the quintessential tapas bar food because they pair as well with cocktails as with wine. For full flavor, do serve them at room temperature. Choose a variety of colors and flavors—purple, brown, green, plump, petite. Picholine, Nicoise, and Calamata become heavenly aromatic after they are marinated overnight in olive oil, crushed garic, orange peel, and hand-torn sprigs of fresh herbs. Garnish with a few spirals of lemon zest. For contrast, serve them with dry-cured California olives or tiny, jewel-like Moroccan black olives. For fun, mix on a platter with various colorful raw vegetables and pickles—and not just the cucumber kind. There are also pickled onions, walnuts, and melon rinds that make a nice addition to an olive spread.

Art Of The Raw Bar

The raw bar packs a visual punch that far outweighs the effort of putting one together. Assemble a variety of containers ranging from galvanized or copper wash-tubs to baking trays and broad, open baskets (lined with plastic). Fill with an ocean of crushed ice. Then decorate with seaweed, edible, pesticide-free flowers, horserad-ish leaves and other tasty edibles from the herb garden. Now you're ready to bring out the fruits of the sea—a smorgasbord of shucked clams and oysters on the half shell, cooked, cold scallops, mussels, and shrimp. Have lots of condiment choices, ranging from spicy cocktail sauce to minced chiles, fresh pepper, lemon and limes for squeezing, horseradish, and a delicate mignonette sauce. Offer buttered black cock-tail bread squares if desired.

The Well-Stocked Bar

It's time to take stock. For a bar that can function smoothly at a cocktail party you'll want to include basic spirits like gin, rum, vodka, tequila, and whiskey—the building blocks of mixed drinks. To treat connoisseurs, you might also have a single-malt Scotch on hand for quaffing. Go with larger, 1-liter bottles for entertaining.

Next up are spirits and wines, such as dry and sweet vermouth, brandy or cognac, and red and white wines that are not too pricey or fussy. In other words, good party drinking wines that everyone can enjoy. Your local liquor store can certainly suggest a few to buy by the case, possibly at a discount. Beer, of course, is also an option—even if you don't plan on making it the focus of your party.

Then it's on to the liqueurs, depending on what you'll be serving: cointreau or triple sec for margaritas, Kahlua for black Russians.

Don't overlook the nonalcoholic ingredients such as juices (cranberry, grapefruit, and orange juices in large bottles); a variety of soft drinks; canned tomato juice or Bloody Mary mix, and of course, club soda, tonic, and bottled water, both still and sparkling.

Condiments and garnishes should round out your liquor cabinet. Lime juice, Angostura bitters, Worcestershire sauce, hot sauce (such as Tabasco), coarse salt, superfine sugar for coating glass rims, cocktail olives, onions, and maraschino cherries.

HOME BAR ESSENTIALS

If you're serious about cocktails, then you'll need these items on hand. Store bar supplies in a cabinet together with the liquor. Also consider a small refrigerator, which comes in handy for wines and vodka, the latter is a particular treat when stored in the freezer.

*Cocktail shaker with strainer
 Metal shaker covers a strainer that fits onto a metal cone

*Electric blender
 For whirling up frozen drinks and crushing ice

*Jiggers
 This helps you measure. With two cones at either end for holding different standard amounts of liquids.

*Bottle opener

*Corkscrew

*Ice buckets, scoops, and tongs

*Pitcher

*Decanter

*Stirrers

GLASS ACTS

The home bartender needs an array of glasses, but not necessarily everything noted on these pages. Since most cocktail recipes do note the type of glassware that should go with it, you'll pretty much always know from reading a recipe what you'll need. Decide what sort of entertaining you'll most likely be doing and outfit your cabinets accordingly.

Above all, the most versatile glass is the cocktail glass. It can easily move from chilled, neat drinks to martinis and frappes. Also known as a martini glass, it's basically just a conical shape and should always be chilled.

Bigger and rounder than the martini glass, the margarita glass is perfect for serving that favorite Mexican drink and has a wide diameter so that you can easily rim it with salt.

You'll also want to have champagne flutes—those familiar tall, tapered glasses designed to keep bubbles bubbly longer because there is a minimum amount of surface area exposed to air. They're also nice for champagne cocktails.

Champagne can also be served in wide-brimmed glasses—the kind that Marilyn Monroe would have used.

Whichever you choose, the champagne glass should be as thin and delicate, since thicker glassware will raise the temperature.

Highball glasses—a.k.a. tumblers—are flat bottomed, plain-looking glasses that hold between eight and twelve ounces. Ideal for mixed drinks, they are generally used for highballs, Tom Collins, bloody Marys, beer, and soda. Lowball glasses (a.k.a. old-fashioneds or on-the-rocks glasses) are also tumblers, but shorter. They hold between five and ten ounces and are also used for mixed drinks like gin-and-tonics, old-fashioneds, black-and-white Russians.

More specialized glassware that you might like to have on hand: Snifters for liqueurs are meant to be cupped in your hand so that your palm actually warms the liquid. They have a classic blown glass shape. Irish coffee glasses have handles for holding hot cocktails like hot buttered rums and hot toddies. Aside from being served in a highball glass, beer is traditionally passed in straight pilsner glasses as well as in English pint glasses.

Though wine can be a complex, complicated subject, wine glasses are the contrary. Keep them plain and simple. Go with the tulip shape, with a wide bowl that tapers toward the top so that it traps aromas. Glasses should have stems for ease of swirling and so that your hand doesn't come in contact with the glass and change the wine's temperature. In other words, always pick up a wine glass by the stem, not the bowl.

Believe it or not, there are no rules set in stone about glasses for red vs. white wine (with the exception of the champagne glass, of course). In general, white wine glasses tend to be a fluted cone shape, while red wine glasses are squatter and more bulbous. Some Europeans drink red wine from tiny little tumblers. Let your aesthetic be your guide.

World of Wine

Traditionally, there is a wine for every food. White wine has long been a favorite partner for seafood, salads, and lighter fare, while red wine goes well with red meats, pasta
dishes, duck, and game. Over the last several years, these rules have been consistently
challenged. Today's thinking overrules these considerations in favor of personal preferences, since the heaviest white wine—for instance, a barrel-aged chardonnay—is
"weightier" than the lightest red wine, such as a Beaujolais or Valpolicella. Still, certain
wines have undeniable affinities for specific foods. And, generally speaking, it's best to go
from light to dark when serving a meal.

White wine, usually produced from white grapes (but not always) should be served
chilled. Common white wine grapes vary greatly. Chardonnay is the sans pareil white
wine grape. The best examples are opulent, lush, rich, and buttery and pair well with
simply prepared chicken, veal, or pork dishes. Less full-bodied than chardonnay,
sauvignon blanc lends itself to many foods; thus, making a good all-purpose wine.
Chenin Blanc, often blended with other grapes, varies from dry or extra sweet. It is
a summertime casual quaffing wine. Riesling, a German wine, tends to be delicate
and sweet (though there are drier versions) and works well as a dessert wine as
well as with Asian dishes. On a similar note, GewÅrztraminer, often left for late harvest to bring out its richness, is often seen as a dessert wine but also works well

with spicy dishes. Muscadet is the quintessential French seafood wine. Semillon is often blended with sauvignon blanc, and Viognier from France is a rich dry wine.

Red wine, by contrast is made from red, purple, or blue grapes. The color comes from the contact with the red grape skins during fermentation. Its flavor tends to be richer and deeper than white wine (indeed, there are wine connoisseurs who don't even recognize white wine as a category!). Served at a warmer temperature than white to let its complex flavors unfold more fully, it can be chilled briefly—say 10 to 15 minutes.

As with white wine, there are many different grapes that go into the mix. One of the best known, cabernet sauvignon, has an intense black currant-and-cedar wood flavor. It works superbly with red meats, especially lamb, and any dish with complex, assertive flavors. Gamay is a lighthearted, berry-tasting wine from France's Beaujolais region that is best enjoyed while young. Grenache is a gorgeous velvety grape that typifies Rhone wines. It works well with strongly flavored foods like grilled sausages or spicy sauces. Merlot, which blends well with cabernet, has a similar flavor profile but softer.

Pinot noir has black cherry, raspberry, and a spicy profile and, when mature, can take on the aroma of game and truffles—it's the quintessential turkey wine. Sangiovese is an Italian bombshell, robust and full-bodied. Syrah/Shiraz (depending on where they're produced) partner pleasingly with game and spicy stews.

Tempranillo is a full-bodied Spanish native that works well with simple grilled meats. It is one of the key grapes of Rioja. With its taste of ripe berries, Zinfandel is the unofficial state grape of California. Use it as you would a cabernet. Rose is a pink-colored wine made when the skin of red grapes is left in contact with the juice for a short period of time. Usually made from the Grenache grape, these pink-tinged wines should be served chilled and complement most anything, especially seafood.

Sparkling wines are created when a yeast and sugar solution is added to dry table wine. The fermentation creates tiny bubbles of carbon dioxide. Only wines produced in the Champagne region of France can be termed Champagne since they are produced using the time-consuming, multi-step method Champenoise. Sparkling wines go by the names Blance de Blanc, Spumante ("sparkling" in Italian), and Cremant.

Inexpensive (But Good) Wines To Try

When you buy by the case, retailers will often shave ten or fifteen percent off prices. Plus, you can sometimes return unopened cases for a refund (check local liquor laws). Tip: Save up to seventy-five percent by choosing a sparkling wine over a true Champagne. And don't think that imports are necessarily more expensive. The following are all reasonably priced nondomestic choices:

Montes Reserve, Sauvignon Blanc, Chile (white)

Marques de Riscal, Rueda, Spain (white)

Palacio de La Vega, Tempranillo Reserva, Spain (red)

Jaume Serra, Cristalino Extra Dry Cava, Spain (sparkling)

Nine Stones McLaren Vale, Shiraz, Australia (red)

Kanu, Chenin Blanc, South Africa (white)

Domaine Houchart, Cìtes de Provence Rose, France (rose)

Sieur d'Arques, Cremant de Limoux Toques & Clochers, France, (sparkling)

Mionetto, IL Prosecco, Italy (sparkling)

Vallebelbo, Moscato d'Asti, Italy (sparkling)

Drink Dressups:

Powdered Sugar, Garnishes, Ribbons, and Charms

*Garnish drinks with lemon balm leaves and curly orange zest

*Add borage flowers, pineapple mint, and curly spearmint to a red punch

*Dip glass rims in lemon juice, then twirl them in colored sugar

*Tie ribbons around the stems—different colors help guests remember which is theirs

*Float cranberries in sparkling water

*Use fun straws

*Customize star fruit wedges in heart shapes using cookie cutters to customize

*Make small glasses out of ice and serve shots in them. Serve with a cotton napkin

*Add scoops of sorbet to ice a drink

*Hollow out plum tomatoes or blood oranges and serve drinks (bloody Marys and mimosas, perhaps) inside, sipped from mini-straws.

Chapter 3. Dinner Party

Do the words "dinner party" strike fear in your heart? Do they bring back memories of being trapped in your childhood room, as the clink of glasses, smells of roast, and chatter of adults drift upward? There is much mystique around the dinner party. A way of entertaining groups with a little more flair than, say, an afternoon cookout, the dinner invitation has a lot of baggage. There is more etiquette associated, more ways to "go wrong."

Not to worry. We've mapped out the proper way to pull it off, even if you don't know a water glass from a red wine goblet. Once you get the hang of it, you'll be throwing parties right and left.

Calm down. Invite your guests into the kitchen to have wine with you. Don't worry about being perfect. And keep your sense of humor. If you're uptight, everyone else will be too. Relax and enjoy yourself. Remember: the ideal number of dinner guests is eight to twelve—just enough to keep the conversation lively and flowing.

Know-How

Choosing A Theme

So much depends on dinner, as the expression goes. But when planning the menu, so much more depends on the season. If you live in a cold, wintry climate, devise ways to enjoy the season with hearty, flavorful foods shared with people you care about. Snuggling by the fire with food and friends is one of the best ways to celebrate the season. Hearty meals designed to fuel outdoor activities like skiing and skating rule. Aside from the holidays, there are a jillion excuses for winter parties: host a sledding or snowman-making party or throw out all the stops for Valentine's Day, the Super Bowl, Mardi Gras, even Elvis's birthday (January 9!)

Come springtime, longer days and a feeling of restless anticipation bring out those "bites of spring," like baby vegetables, lamb, fresh asparagus, and lighter meals. Here is a time of renewal, with parties that emphasize new beginnings. A few excuses: Major League Baseball opening day, a yard sale, Cinco de Mayo, the Kentucky Derby, and, of course, Mother's Day.

Summertime is all about grilling and lounging outdoors. You'll find plenty of suggestions for decorating in the next chapter, but keep in mind that this is all about the bounty of the season: fresh fruits and vegetables, homemade berry ice creams, grilled freshly caught fish with summer vegetables, like corn and zucchini. Summertime themes include the tiki party, Memorial and Labor Day bashes with patriotic touches, pool party (BYOB—bring your own bathing suit).

Of course, autumn is all about bounty—a time of glorious color, crisp, clear air. It's the season to be thinking of stews and soups, of baked parsnips and herbed roasted turkey. Expand your offerings beyond the expected Halloween party to host an Oktoberfest, mark the end of daylight savings time (break out the candles and the hour glasses) and raise a glass to Sadie Hawkins Day (November 13th), when women turn the tables on men.

Planning A Menu

A meal has to function on several levels. On the one hand, it should be nutritious. On the other, it should taste as good as it looks. To achieve this harmony, you'll need to do a little thinking. It's all about balance.

Start with the main course. If you're going with something spicy, like chili or a peppery Mexican dish, side dishes should be considerably milder. However, if the dish is subtly spiced and delicate, the side dishes also shouldn't eclipse it. Think of how to balance your entree with one starch like potatoes, pasta, or rice paired with greens, for instance.

You also need to balance the temperature of the foods—hot and cold. Think also in terms of varied textures, such as crisp with soft. Make sure your meal has a healthy dose of color and interesting shapes. Dessert should also complement the meal. For instance, you wouldn't want to serve brownie sundaes after a four-cheese lasagna. On the other hand, a light meal can end in a rich dessert.

To keep stress levels to a minimum, prepare what you can in advance, go with tried-and-true recipes (no last-minute experimenting!). Unless you'll be having outside help from a caterer or an on-site chef, don't plan a complicated menu. If need be, supplement it with prepared dishes from the local specialty market.

CROWD-PLEASING CLASSICS

Perhaps the most crowd-pleasing, economic, and, above all, versatile dishes around, pastas and risottos are a great bet for a dinner party.

Risotto Revolution

Risotto is the ultimate comfort food of Italy. Chefs never seem to tire of trying new combos. The key to its success is the constant stirring action, which draws out the creaminess and texture of the rice. This is a classic dish for adding new twists. Risottos rely on your choice of stock or cooking liquid absorbed by the rice. Chicken, veal, mushroom, and vegetable stocks are all possibilities. Some chefs have been known to use pure vegetable juice in lieu of stock to intensify the flavor. When making risotto, keep the broth hot so the risotto is simmering at a lively pace.

The six steps to perfect risotto:

1. Have stock simmering on the stove

2. Melt butter

3. Caramelize onions

4. Add rice

5. Add wine and stir until it's been absorbed. Add stock in small increments, stirring until it's absorbed

6. Toss in final ingredients, such as cheese and herbs and any precooked chicken, seafood, and the like

Here are some fun add-ins:

*Pesto with walnuts

*Beet greens with lemon juice

*Sundried tomato or black olive puree

*Shrimp and peas

*Zucchini with fresh basil

Dressing The Table

How to Lay Dinnerware and Flatware

Though the size of the place setting has expanded and contracted over the last two centuries, the number of utensils always corresponds to the number of courses and are arranged from the outside in. That is, place the plate in the center of each place setting. Forks are placed to the left of the plate (except for the very small fish fork, which goes to the right). The spoon and knife, with its blade side turned in toward the plate, go to the right of the plate. Place bread-and-butter plates to the left of the dinner plates just above the forks. If you're serving salad, places plates to the left of the forks.

Depending on your preferences, of course, you could add dessert spoons and forks and coffee spoons horizontally along the top of the plate or just bring them to the table for the dessert course. For French settings, the forks and the soup spoons are deliberately placed upside down to show off the decorations on their backs. As is customary, dessert utensils sit above the plate.

Glassware is arranged left to right in order of size: water, red wine, white wine, dessert wine/sherry. Place them above the knife on the right of the plate. Place cups and saucers to the right behind the glasses. For that final touch, place an attractively folded dinner napkin on or above the dinner plate. It's also correct to fold it in the water glass. If the dinner plates are going to be served warm at the last

minute, simply place the napkin directly on the table.

That having been said, there is an alternative method in which silverware is placed on the table in order of size. Settings look more symmetrical when silverware is placed in order of largest to smallest. This is considered a little more contemporary.

For buffets, which are generally reserved for groups of eight of more, stack dinner plates next to the main course, with side dishes nearby. Place serving utensils, such as salad tongs, alongside the dish. Depending on how the traffic flows, place napkins and flatware at the end of the line or even set actual tables for guests.

Accordingly, you could place glassware on the buffet or on the dining tables. You can definitely improvise with buffets in terms of what goes where. There could be a section for desserts, for instance, or they could go on a separate table.

To stay on schedule, set out everything the night before.

From Pottery to Porcelain

So much mystique surrounds the all-important dinnerware pattern. How to pick the right one? Plain or patterned? Bold colored or neutral? Modern and sleek, country, or traditional?

Before you push the panic button, remember: It's in the mix. You don't have to have a set of all-matching china to set a table. You might mix rustic stoneware with contemporary, deep-hued Asian-look plates in triangles and squares. Pull out your grandmother's fine china and crystal, but mix it up with bamboo and rattan accessories if you so please.

Even with this casual, eclectic attitude, however, it's nice to know the "rules" before you can break them. In other words, know what you're shopping for and then decide how—and if—to mix it up.

When an object is made from fired clay, it is considered a ceramic. Within this category, there is a polyglot of terminology having to do with the type of clay that is used to make the ceramic and the temperature at which it is fired. Among the many subcategories of ceramics are pottery (also known as earthenware) and porcelain, the true china (though now the term is used to describe a broad cross-section of ceramics).

To identify porcelain like a pro, do this test: Hold it up to a bright light. If you can see your fingers on the other side,

then you are likely holding a piece of porcelain. For centuries, porcelain production was a Chinese secret. Then European producers cracked the code in the 18th century. Their first attempts resulted in soft-paste porcelain, which was translucent but not as durable as hard-paste porcelain, which is fired at a higher temperature. Somewhere between hard- and soft-paste porcelain, bone china is yet another variation, said to have been invented by Josiah Spode in the 18th century.

If you were to hold a piece of earthenware up to the light, you'd find that it isn't translucent. It is also more easily broken. Slipware, stoneware, delftware, ironstone, transferware—all are forms of earthenware. Transferware, in particular, is a lot of fun to mix and match in a rainbow of colors—blue, mulberry, black, brown, green, and even polychrome.

Collectors can't get enough of the vividly glazed pottery known as majolica, first introduced in the 1850s by Herbert Minton. Cauliflower-shaped sugar bowls, lettuce-leaf plates, "wicker baskets" filled with fruit molded in relief; realistically decorated seashells resting on painted nests of seaweed...the range of whimsical designs is remarkable and are sure to add personality to your table.

In this century, designs such as chintzware became popular beginning in the 1930s. Printed with tiny flowers all around in the manner of the cloth for which it is named, chintzware adds a delicate look to the tabletop.

The Italian love of long, leisurely meals and spirited conversation gave birth to faience in the mid-16th century. Still going strong, this everyday earthenware decorated with opaque-colored glazes is ever appropriate, easing oh-so-gracefully from lunch to dinner, indoors to out. Blue faience pairs well with a summery cotton striped fabric, as it does with a damask linen cloth.

Silverware

When you think "silver," does a lavish tea service displaying gleaming and polished on a sideboard come to mind? Certainly, it's a pretty picture (if you can afford it), but there's a world of silver out there to collect piece by piece without breaking the budget. Bud vases, toast racks, creamers, marmalade spoons, cake knives, asparagus and sugar tongs, powder jars, pomanders, and salt cellars are among the jumble of silverware you'll typically find at markets, priced so reasonably it's irresistible.

Among the most sought after pieces are British silver and silver-plated items such as napkin rings, teapots, vinaigrettes, and salt cellars. During the last quarter of the nineteenth century, in particular, these objects became imbued with exotic or romantic motifs, such as cupids and other mythological figures. Today, they make charming conversation pieces on the table, particularly on Valentine's Day and other romantic occasions.

Many people shy away from silver collecting, believing that it is too temperamental to clean. But it really isn't all that difficult to care for. Silver that is

marked "sterling " is a standardized alloy of 92.5 percent silver and 7.5 percent copper (or 925 per 1,000 parts pure silver). Silverplate, by contrast, is a base metal that is electroplated with silver.

When true silver turns black, you are seeing silver sulfide—a reaction to humidity as well as sulfurous foods, like eggs, salad dressing, and vinegar. The common sense solution: Clean silver quickly to avoid stains. If possible, keep it in a glass case to minimize humidity. Never store in contact with plastic, which can leave black marks. In fact, acid-free nonabrasive storage materials are essential. To wash, use a mild dishwashing detergent, rinse through, and dry and polish with cotton flannel. To remove tarnish, use only a mild polish, such as a gentle silver foam—forget those "immersion" type cleaners that remove the patina of age. You especially want to show them off in your silver's nooks and crannies.

Love of Linens: How and When to Use Tablecloths, Napkins, Placemats, and Runners

There is no rule specifying that you have to use a tablecloth, placemat, or runner. However, napkins are de rigueur. Dinner napkins are the largest of napkins, measuring about twenty-four inches square at the largest. Napkins for other meals—breakfast and lunch—tend to be smaller by a couple of inches. Cocktail napkins are the tiniest, measuring about four by six inches.

By all means, steer clear of all white. For instance, when you choose a loose-weave linen, playfully ornamented with stripes in an unexpected color like pink, you bring elegance and a relaxed air to the table all at once. Rather than going with an all-white scheme, pair white damask napkins with a tablecloth embroidered with colored thread for a more casual look.

Then there are the many textiles that await creative reuse.

Vintage dish towels with classic red banding are a case in point, particularly the French types, which come in a variety of shapes. The square ones make nice placemats; the longer, narrow types are perfect as table runners. If you find a supply of vintage kitchen linens in similar colors, use them as napkins, perhaps with a classic striped Basque country tablecloth. Drape them over small tables offering hors d'oeuvres, line a tray for a drinks table with them, or tuck them into a basket when you serve muffins and breads. For truly casual meals, bandannas also make good napkins.

Blankets are also perfect table partners. For a cozy winter dinner, toss them over tabletops and strew fringed throws over chair backs. Ticking is a classic rough-and-tumble material also that does well on the table today. Originally a covering for matteresses, linen or cotton ticking is durable and meant to take some wear, which is why it's such a perfect choice for a tablecloth at a summer home, paired with gingham napkins and cheery crockery or china.

Consider, too, the possibilties of fabric from afar. Moroccan, Central American, and Balinese textiles, for instance, all seem to go together. When you combine textiles from various countries, think about the common denominator: color and pattern. Surprisingly, you'll find a strong similairy between African and Scandinavian design in that they both use natural materials, emphasize hand-weaving, and feature strong hues and simple designs. So you could use cloths from Mali and Marimekko alike to cover tables at an outdoor event, each featuring bold color blocks.

Nowadays, a wealth of linens from the past can be had at flea markets, auctions, and estate sales. Among the most captivating and timeless are monogrammed designs, which come from a time when every girl learned stitchery at her mother's knee. When you discover a cache of monogrammed textiles in your antiquing travels, by all means, scoop them up, regardless of the letter they depict or even the purpose they serve. All can be brought to the table with charming results.

For instance, an early 20th century batiste sheet embroidered in high relief with petals and leaves and an initial at center could serve as a tablecloth or even as an outdoor canopy. Monogrammed tea towels from the 1930s could "slipcover" cafe chairs: simply fold them over the tops of the chairs and anchor them with ribbon tied through the hemstitched openings. Initialed cotton handkerchiefs are charming stand-ins for for table napkins. Sturdy ecru linen dishtwels with letters in crosss stitch emboridery make homey placemats.

Candlelight

As professional caterers, restauranteurs, and event planners well know, candles are the least expensive way to transform a room. They are always more dramatic in a large group, and you can multiply their effect by setting them on a mirror or placing them on a mantel over the fireplace with a mirrored background. In fact, you can decorate with a whole glittering constellation of candlesticks of different sizes and materials: crystal, glass, metal, pottery. To unite them all, use the same candle in each, perhaps a classic ivory-toned beeswax taper.

Also rummage in your cupboards for alternatives. Celery holders, hurricane glass chimneys, and footed ice cream dishes make for an intriguing display. Eggcups and orphaned teacups are perfect for votives, while flowerpots turned upside down and fitted with tapers in the drainage hole are quick yet imaginative tabletop solutions.

You might even dress up candle holders with tiny necklaces of crafts store beads strung on wire. When you group a variety of candles in related colors together, you're guaranteed a pretty look. Go ahead and mix crystal, metal, and ceramic holders. To create a mesmerizing mood for an evening gathering, pair all-white candles with pale flowers, which will seem to glow in the dark.

More possibilities: Float votives in a pottery punchbowl and set on the kitchen counter, a pedestal table, or a wooden crate. Floating candles also look wonderful bobbing in a collection of clear glass cylinders. In wintertime, bring the display outdoors with glowing lanterns. Candles decorated with foliage, hot glued in place, wink and gleam on a silver tray, which can be transported anywhere for instant aura. Displayed on a tiered stand, honeycomb votives, roses, and white turnips draw guests to a wine and cheese buffet.

Not Just Flowers: Ideas For Centerpieces And Place Settings

First, know that there is absolutely no rule on the books that says a tabletop must have a crystal fruitbowl flanked by two candlesticks.

A collection of wooden spools of varying sizes makes for an architectural tablescape. Arrange a collection of colored glassware down the center of a table in a serpentine fashion. Display a collection of found natural objects on top—moss, acorns, pods, and stones. A shallow pewter bowlful of carpet balls with a red and white theme makes a cheery accent.

Bring freesia and tuberoses in vases to share the table with pots of rosemary and passionflower. Place little pots of herbs on a tiered etagere. A tableside baker's rack filled with canning jars holding tuberoses will charm as much as a centerpiece. Or simply float blossoms in footed bowls. Think jasmine, lemon flowers, and gardenias.

Nonfloral Centerpieces

Feather boas are fun and funky. They're especially useful if you have a color scheme that's hard to create in flowers—for instance, black and white. White flowers combine with black feathers.

Fruits and nuts create a Dutch still-life look. Small, delicate fruits like kumquats and little acorns and pinecones, even strawberries look pretty with flowers.

Use mirrors to extend the arrangement, whether underneath or behind to double the effect.

March eucalyptus leaves down the table's center, interspersed with seasonal fruits like pomegranates, pears, and persimmons

Whatever you choose, keep the centerpiece low so that guests can see each other, which stimulates conversation.

Use flowers, to be sure, but mix them with fruits like persimmons and pears.

Chapter 4. Holidays

Entertaining takes on a grander dimension when it's centered on holidays. Rather than merely serving a meal, you'll be creating memories and carrying on nostalgic childhood traditions, perhaps with your own twist.

There are a number of simple strategies to make your life easier during this potentially stressful time. In planning the menu, go with simple-to-prepare recipes. Your old favorites will work perfectly, so long as they're presented with panache. Or plan on updating a standard recipe with a new twist, like a sprightly fruit sauce instead of traditional gravy. Prepare as much as you can a day or two in advance. That way, on the day of the party, you'll only need to reheat dishes or making simple side dishes.

Well before the day arrives, take inventory of tables and seating. If your dining table isn't long enough to serve as a buffet, use the kitchen island instead. Or plan on putting a door on sawhorses and cover with an attractive tablecloth. Ask friends and neighbors for folding chairs if you think you'll need extra seating, or rent them from a party-supply house.

The night before, set out platters and serving bowls to guide traffic flow. Place large plates near entree dishes and smaller plates near side dishes or appetizers. Set up a beverage station on its own table.

On the day of, don't go it alone. Let the whole family get involved. Teenage children could serve as waiters and candle lighters, while younger kids could greet guests and take their coats to a coatroom. They could also have fun dressing up the family pet to greet guests at the door.

Open-House Tree Trimming

It's a lot of fun to get everyone involved in trimming the tree. You'll find your kids even more engaged in the process if cousins or friends are on hand. Or maybe your decorating style needs a breath of fresh air and could benefit from the input of holiday guests. By all means, invite a crew of all ages and pull out all the stops to make them feel welcome.

Establish a welcoming note by lighting the way with luminaries made from ordinary brown lunch bags. Simply fill with one inch of sand and add a votive candle. They'll provide beacons of cheer on a dark winter's night while also lighting the way for arriving and departing guests.

Rather than limit decorations to the living room, sprinkle them through practically every room of your home. Ordinary household objects need only minor additions twist to shine. When you fill teacups, trophies, and compotes with vintage glass tree ornaments or collectible figural glass light bulbs in the shapes of Santas and snowmen, they instantly get into the holiday spirit. Even if you don't have vintage col

lectibles on hand, you can still create a memorable setting.

Classic tissue paper snowflakes could decorate windows, while paper partridges perch in a reproduction feather tree. Paper chain garlands created from gift wrap could decorate mantels, banisters, and powder room windows with plenty of charm.

On Christmas Morning...

If you have overnight guests for the holidays, set them a special breakfast table. Pile a tiered stand high with kumquats, pomegranates, and other appealing fruits nestled among shiny ornaments. Make each place setting special with green napkins cinched with mandarin-colored ribbons. Equally festive are napkin rings made from strands of prestrung glass beads or flatware simply tied with a silver ribbon.

Just for the fun of it, offer a diner-style menu you've printed up on the computer. It could be decorated with stamped images and bound with holiday ribbons—or let the kids create their own. Use cookie molds to make tree- or wreath-shaped pancakes ornamented with strawberry "bows."

Wreaths, Garlands, and Display Ideas

Southerners and Californians have long known that you can get that Christmas feeling without the usual suspects of holly and ivy. Instead, French flower buckets overflowing with pineapples, baskets of citrus, and pots of paper whites and ornamental cabbages encircling the tree (or a sled and Adirondack chair) get you in a natural mood while a simple concoction of cinnamon sticks, clove and allspice simmers with water on the stove. A planter filled with hyacinth pots nestled neck-deep in moss with pyracantha berries spilling over the sides is a far cry from the expected poinsettias.

Instead of the usual citrus clove pomander, try one gleaming with beadwork or turned into a votive holder. Down-to-earth decorations include eucalyptus banister garlands entwined with safflower pods, ferns, and lemon leaves or humble glass containers wrapped in raw silk and festooned with fresh roses and snow berries from the yard. For a fresh-from-the-woods look, swag grapevines over doorways accented with sprigs of cockscomb and dried floral bundles. Trim the tree with cranberry stars or chicken wire everlasting bouquets and swath it in a burlap tree skirt in a petal shape.

There are so many fresh ways to go: Grass green and peony pink gift wrap...cards strung on jute roping, interspersed with jingle bells, pinecones, and pomegranates...votives tucked into hollowed-out apples or artichokes set on the windowsill...a make-it-yourself holly topiary dangling with gilded cardboard fruits or favorite seashells...corrugated paper gift wrap festooned with tiny pine cones...faux floral "collars" for lampshades...potato print stockings ...birch branches coaxed into a wreath and dusted with gold glitter.

Orange Chicken Breasts with Pomegranate

Pomegranates are in season just around the holidays, so the next time you're having a crowd over, consider this healthy, flavorful dish instead of the usual turkey or ham. This recipe serves 6 as a main course or 12 as a light buffet offering.

Marinade:

1 cup freshly squeezed orange juice (about 3 large oranges)

4 tablespoons Aurum (an Italian liqueur), orange liqueur, or cognac

Grated zest of 2 oranges

½ teaspoon freshly grated nutmeg

¼ teaspoon ground cardamom (optional)

Entree:

6 whole boneless, skinless chicken breasts, halved

Salt and freshly ground pepper to taste

Flour for dredging

1 egg, beaten

Fine, dry bread crumbs

Olive oil

Canola oil

2 tablespoons sweet (unsalted) butter

Grated zest of 1 orange

Seeds of 1 pomegranate

Chopped Italian (flat-leaf) parsley for garnish

Mix all the marinade ingredients together in a glass bowl and marinate the chicken for at least an hour. Drain and reserve the marinade. Pat the chicken dry with paper towels and season with salt and pepper to taste.

Dredge the breasts in flour and shake off any excess. Dip in the egg. Let the excess drip off, and coat each piece with bread crumbs. Pour equal amounts of each oil into a sauté pan to a depth of ¼ inch and heat on medium heat. Sauté the chicken on both sides until brown and cooked through, about 5 minutes per side.

Remove the chicken to a serving dish and keep warm. After all the breasts are cooked, discard the oil and add the butter, reserved marinade, and orange zest to the pan. Bring to a boil over high heat and reduce until the mixture thickens, about three minutes. Add the pomegranate seeds and season with salt and pepper. Pour the sauce over the chicken, sprinkle with parsley, and serve.

One of the fun activities could also be coloring eggs. There are a couple of ways to go:

*Substitute icing coloring (such as Wilton Icing Colors) for food coloring to achieve richer colors than you'd get with traditional Easter egg dyes. Brown eggs especially lend themselves to this look.

*Go natural: Onion skins tied around eggs give an orange marbled effect. Or create a dye bath from beets and cranberries for pink and red, spinach for delicate green.

*Achieve plaids and stripes by wrapping your oeufs in rubber bands, dental floss, and strips of narrow masking tape Alternatively, stamp with potato blocks and ink or poster paint.

*Layer colors by dipping eggs into progressively deeper shades. Rub with mineral oil for a soft sheen.

*Vary egg sizes. Go small with speckled quail eggs. Duck and goose eggs are double and triple the size of hen's eggs, respectively. Larger still, rhea, emu, and ostrich eggs are all sturdy enough to be carved and etched with a dremel tool and look great with metallic finishes. Emu eggs come already colored emerald green.

*Display them in a basket as your centerpiece, whether an old metal egg basket or an herb gathering type. Alternatively, nestle them in a graniteware bowl.

Thanksgiving

A Work Plan

Some would argue that the holidays that are completely devoted to food—and not gift giving—are the best of all. One of the best ways to savor Thanksgiving, of course, is as a potluck where everyone contributes a dish. Still, if you're the lucky host you'll need to do a little more advance planning than usual. The weekend before, you'll want to get out the serving dishes you'll need. Read through all the recipes to make sure you have all the ingredients you'll need. Make any soups you plan on serving. The day before, bake casseroles and prepare vegetable side dishes as well as desserts. On the morning of, prepare your turkey for the oven and set the dinner table after breakfast. In the afternoon, complete and warm up your side dishes, make gravy, and enjoy!

Freezing Tips:

*Equip your freezer with a thermometer so that you can do periodic temperature checks. It should read 0 degrees.

 *Since liquid expands as it freezes, leave extra room—about one inch—in soup and stew containers when going into the freezer.

*Thaw foods in the refrigerator for safety's sake. Defrosting at room temperature can lead to bacterial growth and spoilage.

*If you know you're going to cook food and put it directly in the freezer for later usage, undercook it slightly. That way, when you're reheating it you can cook it longer without overcooking it.

Turkey Talk

When buying turkey, figure on about 1 pound per person. The younger the turkey, the more tender the meat. Wild turkeys are another great option; your local butcher might be able to arrange one for you if you discuss it well in advance.

Before roasting turkey, remove the giblets (they are in the body or neck cavity) neck and liver. You can use the giblets and neck for stock, while the liver would be good cooked in a stuffing.

To prepare the bird, rinse and pat it dry, inside and out, using paper towels. Put it on a platter, covered, to catch juices. The United States Department of Agriculture (USDA) recommends buying a fresh turkey no more than 2 days before you're ready to use it and not defrosting frozen turkey until you're ready to use it. For frozen turkey defrosted in the refrigerator, allow one day of thawing for every four to five pounds of turkey. The USDA also suggests roasting at 325 degrees or higher, and checking the internal temperature with a meat thermometer. A cautious cook's rule of thumb: When the thickest part of the thigh reaches 180 degrees F on the thermometer, the turkey is done. Do not go by the color of the cooked meat, as it is not a surefire way to test doneness. After roasting, a turkey should stand for 15 to 20 minutes. This allows the juice to congeal and make carving a bit easier. Check the USDA website for up-to-date turkey tips www.fsis.usda.gov.

Autumn Decor

Thanksgiving tabletops don't have to be all turkeys and Pilgrims. Try a cabin in the woods theme. Line up a row of balsam-incense-burning log cabins you see at country gift shops. They look especially homey paired with a large-checked tablecloth.

Set up a Thanksgiving table with a variety of seasonal vegetables and wild things gathered from the woods. In addition to gourds, pumpkins, and squashes, try using mosses on a plate as a centerpiece, topped with acorns and honey locust pods. Set out woven baskets filled with pinecones and nuts.

Hollow out pumpkins as candleholders for a harvest celebration; for added color, cluster Savoy cabbages in rich mossy greens and electric purples. Fill a clear glass pantry jar with clementines.

For an intriguing centerpiece, consider bittersweet vines, which have naturally beautiful curves. Dynamic twists of this wild vine would make a surprising contrast with the serenity of a cultivated flower, such as peach-tinged white roses. Place in a container woven from palm fibers for even more textural contrast. Another option is to lay a

Menu

Appetizer

Balsamic Glazed Quail stuffed with Sun Dried Tomatoes
and Wild Mushrooms
French Lentil and Chorizo Ragout

Salad

Merlot Poached French Butter Pear with Maytag
Blue Cheese, Baby Frisee and Honey Gastrique

Entrée

Grilled Filet Mignon with Chilean Sea Bass,
Black Truffle Mashed Potatoes, Sun Dried Tomato Olive
Tapenade, Grilled Vegetables

Viennese Dessert Tab...

Bananas Foster prepared to order with Vanil...
Chocolate Sacher Torte, Dulce de Lech...
Chestnut St. Honor...
Fresh Fruit Tarts & Coconut C...
Chocolate Truffles & Double...

Coffee Service, Cappu...

grapevine wreath directly at the table's center. Combine herbs, tiny spears of red sumac, and chile peppers on the base. Don't cover it completely—the base is meant to show. By contrast, foam or straw wreaths work well with cranberries and rosehips because you can simply attach them by cutting toothpicks in half and using them to skewer berries to the wreath. Another option is to use floral glue. If you are using larger elements on such wreaths, such as apple, lay down a base of ivy leaves or some other foliage to camouflage the base completely. Decorate the sideboard with a huge dried gourd.

Round out the look with nature-inspired napkin rings. Assemble clusters of eucalyptus, autumn leaves, cinnamon sticks, and dried sage. Tie the aromatic bundles together and cinch around a napkin with raffia for a rustic look. For truly festive placecards, write guests' names in gold craft paint on bay leaves, tie a napkin with a lush velvet ribbon, and tuck each leaf inside. Another fun touch: Use a bay leaf coated with gold textile paint as a "stamp" for napkins.

Cranberry Nachos

Here's an appetizer that gives Thanksgiving cranberries a completely new twist. The nacho chips laden with red and yellow pepper coulis, cranberry salsa, and goat cheese are arranged on a plate around a radicchio leaf "bowl" filled with still more cranberry salsa.

Red and Yellow Pepper Coulis (¼ cup each)

1 whole yellow bell pepper

1 whole red bell pepper

4 tablespoons olive oil

Salt and freshly ground pepper to taste

Cranberry Salsa:

½ cup cranberries

¼ cup fresh orange juice

¼ medium red onion, diced

1 fresh jalapeno pepper, diced

2 tablespoons chopped cilantro

¼ cup fresh lime juice

Pinch salt

Freshly ground pepper to taste

Sugar to taste

Nachos:

12 blue and gold tortilla chips

¼ pound mild goat cheese (chevre)

Radicchio

4 sprigs cilantro

Red and Yellow Pepper Coulis:

Char the whole peppers open over an open flame or under a preheated broiler. Place in a metal bowl and cover tightly with plastic wrap. Let sit for 15 minutes. Then wash off all charred skin and puree in 2 batches (one for each pepper) in the food processor until smooth. Drizzle olive oil over each coulis batch and season with salt and pepper.

Sources & Suppliers

Speciality Foods
Meat & Game

D'Artagnan
www.dartagnan.com
(800) 327-8246
marinated duck breast

The HoneyBaked Ham Company
www.honeybaked.com
(866) 492-HAMS

Lobel's
www.lobels.com
(877) 783-4512
natural prime beef

Sam's Butcher Shop
www.samsbutchershop.com
(570) 842-9707
specialty meats

Fish & Seafood

Bold Coast Smokehouse
www.boldcoastsmokehouse.com
(888) 733-0807
Scandinavian gravlax, smoked lox

Browne Trading Company
www.brownetrading.com
(800) 944-7848

Perona Farms
www.peronafarms.com
(800) 750-6190
smoked Atlantic salmon

Oils, Vinegars & Preserves

Anamarie Organic Olive Oil
www.anamarieorganicoliveoil.com
(845) 635-2530
Portuguese olive oil, olives, vinegars

Chef Shop
www.chefshop.com
(800) 596-0885

Gustiamo
www.gustiamo.com
(877) 907-2525
citrus marmalades

Stonewall Kitchen
www.stonewallkitchen.com
(800) 207-JAMS

Cheese

Cow Girl Creamery
www.cowgirlcreamery.com
(866) 433-7834
organic artisan cheeses

Mozzarella Company
www.mozzco.com
cow's and goat's milk cheeses, samplers
(800) 798-2954

Sprout Creek Farm
www.sproutcreekfarm.org
(845) 485-9885
farm-made European-style cheeses

Savory Treats

Bella Cucina Artful Food
www.bellacucina.com
(800) 580-5674
Italian foods

Farm Country Soups
www.farmcountrysoup.com
(866) 877-SOUP
elegant, dinner-party-quality soups

Frog Hollow Farm
www.froghollow.com
(888) 779-4511
turnovers in many flavors; also fresh fruit

Hancock Gourmet Lobster Company
www.hancockgourmetlobster.com
(800) 552-0142
elegant lobster rolls

Ruthie & Gussie's
www.ruthieandgussies.com
(877) 4-LATKES
traditional potato pancake batter for Hanukkah and beyond...

Dessert

Dancing Deer Baking Co.
www.dancingdeer.com
(888) 699-DEER
brownies, gingerbread cake, mixes

David Bouley
www.davidbouley.com
(212) 964-2525
lemon tea cake

Empire Torte Company
www.empiretorte.com
(800) 908-6783
intense chocolate tortes

My Boulangerie
myboulangerie.com
(360) 421-1618
authentic French pastries and croissants

Polly's Cakes
www.pollyscakes.com
(888) 386-1221
cakes